TABLE OF CONTENTS

T0024112

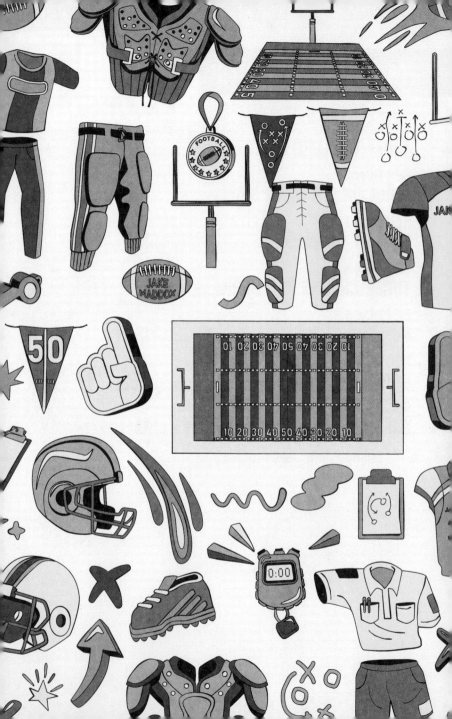

SECTION 1:
TEAM TICKLERS

When is a football player like a metal worker?

When he's a Pittsburgh Steeler.

5

When is a football player like a black bird?

When he's a Baltimore Raven.

When is a football player as big as a bison?

When he's a Buffalo Bill.

When is a football player like a tiger?

When he's a Cincinnati Bengal.

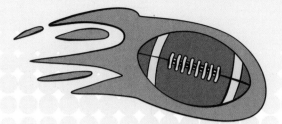

When is a football player like a wild horse?

When he's a Denver Bronco.

When is a football player like a young horse?

When he's an Indianapolis Colt.

When is a football player like the largest cat in North America?

When he's a Jacksonville Jaguar.

When is a football player like a warrior who attacks someone by surprise?

When he's a Las Vegas Raider.

When is a football player like an American revolutionary?

When he's a New England Patriot.

When is a football player like a sleek sea mammal?

When he's a Miami Dolphin.

When is a football player like a bright red bird?

When he's an Arizona Cardinal.

When is a football player like a bird of prey?

When he's an Atlanta Falcon, a Philadelphia Eagle, or a Seattle Seahawk!

When is a football player like a black wildcat?

When he's a Carolina Panther.

What kind of football player hibernates in winter?

A Chicago Bear.

When is a football player like the king of the jungle?

When he's a Detroit Lion.

When is a football player like a mountain goat?

When he's a Los Angeles Ram.

When is a football player like a Scandinavian seafarer?

When he's a Minnesota Viking.

Which football team is the holiest?

The New Orleans Saints.

When is a football player like a pirate?

When he's a Tampa Bay Buccaneer.

When is a football player like a gold rush prospector?

When he's a San Francisco 49er.

When does a quarterback say "fe, fi, fo, fum!" instead of "hut, hut, hike?"

When he's a New York Giant.

Which football team is like a group of men on horseback?

The Dallas Cowboys.

Which football team is like a packaging company?

The Green Bay Packers.

Which football team flies across the field the fastest?

The New York Jets.

What happens when you mix the Cleveland Reds, the Cleveland Yellows, and the Cleveland Blues together?

You get the Cleveland Browns.

What do you call a football player in a 10-gallon hat and cowboy boots?

A Houston Texan.

Which football team is descended from ancient Greek giants?

The Tennessee Titans.

Which football team helps keep laptops and phones at full power?

The Los Angeles Chargers.

Which football team likes to be in charge of things?

The Kansas City Chiefs.

WALK ON THE WILD SIDE

Why was the game between the Carolina Panthers and Chicago Bears so intense?

They were fighting fang and nail!

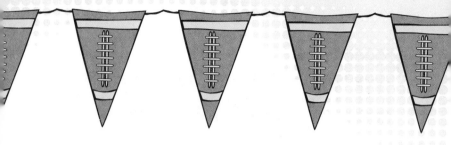

What did the bee say after it made a touchdown?

"Hive scored!"

Why didn't the dog want to play football?

Because it was a boxer.

What do you call a touchdown by a Tyrannosaurus rex?

A dino-*score*!

Where do the Jacksonville Jaguars practice?

At the jungle gym.

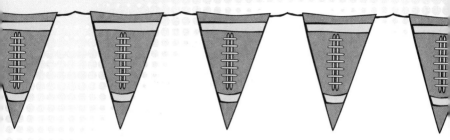

Why wouldn't the coach let the pig play football?

Because it was a ball hog.

Do you know why football coaches don't like pigs?

Because they play dirty.

What should you do when you see a rhino with a football?

Get out of its way!

Why should you never play football at the zoo?

Because there are too many cheetahs.

Why did the elephants get jobs at the football stadium?

They liked working for peanuts.

Why did the Philadelphia Eagles fly south for the winter?

Because it was too far to walk there.

What do Miami Dolphins players wear instead of cleats?

Squeakers.

Why did the Dallas Cowboys lasso the Indianapolis Colts?

They wanted to tie up the score.

Which football play do dogs love the most?

The flea flicker.

How do the Detroit Lions line up on the field?

In the wildcat formation.

Did you hear that grasshoppers don't like football?

They prefer cricket.

Which football game is a cat's favorite?

The Fish Bowl.

Which insect is not good at playing football?

The fumble bee!

What do you call a bunch of Bengals in a circle?

The huddle.

Why did the chicken cross the field?

To get to the other sideline.

Why do dogs make terrible coaches?

Because they hound their players.

What's the difference between a running back and a duck?

One goes *quick* and the other goes *quack*.

How are football teams like crocodiles?

They both have long snappers.

How did the Bengal change his stripes?

He got traded to another team.

Which arachnid is good at playing football?

A *score*-pion!

What do you call a monkey that wins the Super Bowl?

A *chimp*-ion!

How do you stop squirrels from playing football in your yard?

Hide the ball. It drives them nuts!

Why did the chicken run onto the football field?

The ref was calling fowls.

Why did the pig playing football need a medic?

He pulled his ham string.

Why did the centipede football player miss the first half?

He was putting on his shoes.

Why are losing football teams like smashed tomatoes?

Because they have to ketchup!

Why do chickens make great cheerleaders?

Because they like to egg their team on!

Did you hear about the player who got cut from the team for doing an illegal move?

It was okay, though. He got a job working as a butcher. He put his chop block to good use!

Where did the offensive lineman stack his flapjacks?

On his pancake block.

Why did the coach ask the quarterback to cook her eggs?

Because she was a great scrambler.

How do the Los Angeles Chargers stay hydrated?

With energy drinks that are full of *electro*-lytes!

What do cheerleaders drink before each game?

Root beer!

Why did the players bring ice cream to practice?

They heard there would be cones on the field.

Did you hear about the football team that forgot their coach's birthday cake?

They made up for it by icing the kicker!

Why don't concession stands at stadiums have snail on the menu?

Because they only serve fast food.

Why does the Packers' stadium smell like dairy products?

Because of all the cheeseheads.

Why do bakers like to watch football between the 20-yard line and the goal line?

Because it's the bread zone.

Where do hungry football players play?

In the Supper Bowl!

What kind of pastry do defensive backs eat at the game?

Turnovers.

Why did the coach put lettuce on the field?

His team needed to get a head.

Why do football players like hot dogs?

They're great for both losers and wieners!

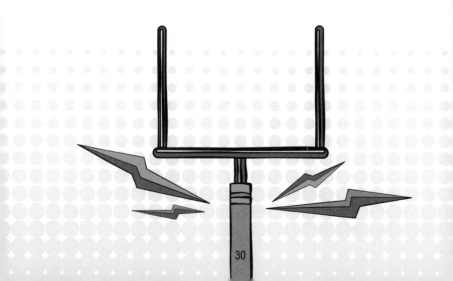

What do quarterbacks like to do at dinner?

Pass the salt.

What has 44 legs and goes crunch, crunch, crunch?

Two football teams eating chips on the field.

What did the dad potato say to his son playing football?

I'm rooting for you!

THREE CHEERS FOR GEAR

How did the football player block the dentist?

She used her mouth guard.

When do football players wear suits of armor?

During knight games.

Why did the football leave the field during the game?

It was tired of being kicked around.

Which football player wears the biggest helmet?

The one with the biggest head, of course!

Which football player wears the biggest cleats?

The one with the biggest feet!

How do football players keep their jerseys wrinkle-free?

They use the *gridiron*.

How do football players wash their cleats?

In *running* water.

Which shirt does the kicker wear when she wants to balance the ball?

Her *tee*-shirt.

What did the wide receiver's hands say when he caught the football?

I glove you!

Why are football players under so much pressure?

They wear tight uniforms.

Did you hear the news? The quarterback's jacket just quit.

I guess it was getting too much flak!

Why did the Los Angeles Rams coach tell his players to put on their helmets?

Because they were always head-butting things.

Did you hear about the team that lost the championship?

It's okay. They held their heads up high—by their chin straps!

Did you know that football players' socks have holes in them?

Of course they do! How else would they get their feet in them?

What's as big as the Heisman Trophy but weighs nothing?

The trophy's shadow.

What kind of shoes do centers wear?

Hiking shoes.

How are football players always ready for Halloween?

Because they're always wearing face masks.

Why does the Vikings locker room have a tiny vending machine?

It has Mini-sodas!

Why did the football player fail his test?

He was a tackling dummy.

What thing on the football field is not having any fun?

The score bored.

SECTION 5:
PUN FUN

What do football players drink at a cold game?

Hot penal-tea!

Did you hear that a football game is only worth a dollar?

Yeah, because it's made up of four quarters.

Did you hear about the coach who took her clock out to her yard?

She wanted a timeout.

Why is it always breezy at a football game?

Because the stadium is full of fans.

What is a quarterback's favorite pastime?

Going for a hike.

Why did the wide receiver dive into the pool?

The quarterback told him to go deep.

Why are quarterbacks such good students?

Because they're always passing.

Why did the losing team bring rope onto the field?

To tie up the score.

What did the defensive back say to the ball after the game?

"Catch you later!"

When are defensive players offensive?

When they cross the line (of scrimmage).

Which football team would you find at the top of a beanstalk?

The Giants.

Which football team carries the most luggage when traveling?

The Packers.

Which state provides new uniforms for football teams?

New Jersey.

Knock, Knock?
Who's there?

Woo.
Woo who?

Why are you cheering?
We just lost the game!

Wide Receiver: Knock, Knock!

Tight End: Who's there?

Wide Receiver: Wide.

Tight End: Wide who?

Wide Receiver: Wide you lock me out?!

How do astronauts play football in outer space?

On Astro-turf!

What runs all around the field but never moves?

The fence.

Why are football practices always so noisy?

Because of all the drills.

What is black and white and barks at the players?

The *ruff*-eree!

What is harder for the running back to catch the more she runs?

Her breath.

What happens when the Chicago Bears get caught in the rain?

They become Drizzly Bears.

Knock, Knock!
Who's there?

Arizona Cardinals go.
Arizona Cardinals go who?

Arizona Cardinals don't go "Who!" Owls do!

How do chickens gather in a football huddle?

They go cluck-wise.

Which Ohio team was left out in the freezing cold?

The Cleveland *Brrrr*-owns.

How did the Miami Dolphins feel after winning the game?

Fin-tastic!

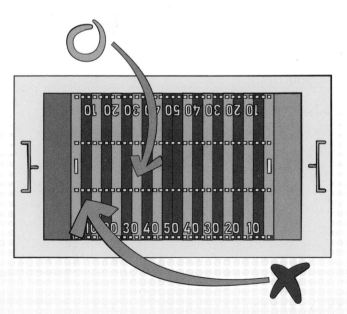

Did you hear about the coach who let his bloodhound play for his team?

It played scenter.

What's the difference between a thunderstorm and an injured Detroit Lion?

One pours with rain. The other roars with pain.

What do you call the Cardinals mascot, Big Red, when he teases the other team?

A mockingbird.

What do you call the Texans' mascot, Toro, when he's sleeping?

A bull-dozer!

Where does a Seattle Seahawk go when he's sick?

To the dock.

What do the New York Giants and the New York Jets have in common?

The same first name.

Why does the Rams mascot, Rampage, wear a bell around his neck?

Because his horns don't work.

How do the Tampa Bay Buccaneers communicate on the field?

Aye to aye.

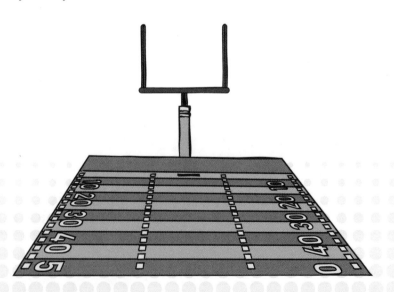

How much did the Tampa Bay players pay for their piercings?

About a buck an ear.

Why did the referee send the football player camping?

He was being penalized for roughing.

When is a football player most focused during the game?

When he is in *the zone*.

What do you call a Green Bay Packers cheese hat that isn't yours?

Nacho cheese.

Why won't the coach let his all-star team listen to music?

Because they keep breaking records.

Why is the stadium so hot after the game?

Because all the fans have left.

Which team went to jail for theft?

The Pittsburgh *Steal*-ers.

SECTION 6:
COACH'S CHUCKLES

How did the punter break her bad habit?

She was able to kick it!

51

Why did the football need to calm down?

It was spiraling out of control.

Which player is the sharpest on the team?

The cornerback.

Why was the player's helmet radio pulling in lots of static?

There was too much interference from the other team.

Why did the coach make the calamari the Most Valuable Player?

Because of its *squid* kick.

Football players make great fishermen.

They know how to hook and tackle.

Football players are also great problem-solvers.

They tackle things head-on.

When is a quarterback like a bunch of potatoes?

When he gets sacked.

What's black and white and red all over?

A referee with a sunburn.

Why is a football field the safest place to be?

Because there are so many guards.

What's the hardest thing about playing in the Super Bowl?

The ground.

Did you hear about the joke the quarterback told her receivers?

It flew right over their heads.

I got lost on the way to the stadium, so I stopped for directions. "How do you get to the Super Bowl?" I asked. Know what they told me?

"Lots of practice!"

What's a New Yorker's favorite football play?

The Statue of Liberty.

What is a mouse's favorite football play?

The quarterback squeak!

What is the Buccaneers' special alphabet lineup called?

The Aye Formation.

How did the quarterback win the game during the thunderstorm?

With a *Hail* Mary pass.

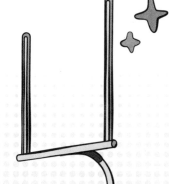

Which outside running play requires a broom?

The running back sweep.

Why couldn't the quarterback kill the vampire?

He used a fake spike!

Why did the coach think the locker room was haunted?

He could hear the team's spirit echoing from the walls.

How does a ghost score a field goal?

He kicks the ball through the *ghoul* post.

How do you know when the Chargers are winning?

Because the crowd is electrified!

What did the mummy coach tell his players in the fourth quarter?

Let's wrap this up!

Why did the angry coach break the referee's phone?

The ref made a bad call.

Why does the center find playing football so easy?

He thinks it's a *snap!*

When is a cornerback or safety like five cents?

When they are a nickelback.

Why did the coach go to the bank?

Because he wanted his quarterback.

When are the Jets most like an air raid?

When they blitz.

When is a football team like a landing airplane?

When they get a touchdown.

Why did the football players toss around the clock?

They wanted to pass the time.

What did the football say to the punter?

"I get a kick out of you."

Where do football players dance?

At the Foot Ball.

What do you call a bunch of football fans in the basement when their team is losing?

A whine cellar.

Where does a retired quarterback go?

Out to *pass*-ture.

Why did the poor quarterback make his receivers cross mid field?

He was trying to make the (defensive) ends meet.

What do you call an offensive lineman's kid?

A chip off the old blocker!

What do you call a boat full of polite football players?

A good sportsman-*ship*!

Where do football players go shopping?

At the tackle shop.

What happens when a lazy quarterback takes a test?

He doesn't pass.

Who are the happiest people at a football game?

The cheerleaders.

What did the coach do when the field flooded?

He sent in his subs.

Why did the punt returner marry his girlfriend?

She was a fair catch.

What do you call it when the defense pulls the ball from an offensive player in a funny way?

A comic strip.

ONE-LINER LAUGHS

I didn't know who had the ball.

And then it hit me!

Old quarterbacks don't die.

They just *pass* away.

I've tried giving up on football.

But I couldn't *kick* the habit.

Which football players can jump higher than a goalpost?

All of them—goalposts can't jump!

Peter Pan can't play quarterback.

His throws Never Land.

People who wear eyeglasses can't play football.

It's a *contact* sport.

The easiest target to hit with a football . . .

. . . is the *wide* receiver.

When is a football player like a judge?

When he sits on the bench.

Why was the chicken ejected from the game?

Because of his *fowl* play!

What do the most successful kickers do?

They always reach their goals.

Why are losing teams like scrambled eggs?

They both get beaten.

How are coaches like punters?

They always put their best foot forward.

Why couldn't the skeleton play football?

His heart just wasn't in it.

Why did the baby ghost join the football team?

Because they needed a little team spirit.

What is the undertaker's favorite part of the football field?

The end zone.

TELLING FUNNY JOKES!

1. Know your joke.
Be sure you memorize the whole joke before you tell it. Most of us have heard someone start a joke by saying, "Oh, this is SO funny . . ." But then they can't remember part of it. Or they forget the ending, which is the most important part of the joke—the punch line!

2. Speak up.
Don't mumble your words. And don't speak too fast or too slow. Just speak clearly. You don't have to use a strange voice or accent. (Unless that's part of the joke!)

3. Look at your audience.
Good eye contact with your listeners will grab and hold their attention.

4. Don't overthink things.
You don't need to use silly gestures to tell your joke, unless it helps sell the punch line. You can either sit or stand to tell your jokes. Make yourself comfortable. Remember, telling jokes is basically just talking to people to make them laugh.

5. Don't laugh at your own joke.
Sure, comedians sometimes crack up laughing while they're telling a story. And that can be pretty funny by itself. But normally, it's best not to laugh at your own jokes. If you do, you might lose the timing of your joke or mess it up. Let your audience do the laughing. Your job is to be the funny one.

6. Practice your setup.

The setup is the second most important part of a joke. This includes everything you say before getting to the punch line. Be as clear as you can so when you reach the punch line, it makes sense!

7. Get the punch line right.

The punch line is the most important part of the joke. It's the payoff to the main event. A good joke is best if you pause for a second or two before delivering the punch line. That tiny pause will make your audience pay attention, eager to hear what's coming next.

8. Practice, practice, practice.

Practice your routine until you know it by heart. You can also watch other comedians or a comedy show or film. Listen to other people tell a joke. Pay attention to what makes them funny. You can pick up skills by seeing how others get an audience laughing. With enough practice, you'll soon be a great comedian.

9. It's all about the timing.

Learn to get the timing right for the biggest impact. Waiting for the right time and giving that extra pause before the punch line can really zing an audience. But you should also know when NOT to tell a joke. You probably know when your friends like to hear something funny. But when around unfamiliar people, you need to "read the room" first. Are people having a good time? Or is it a more serious event? A joke is funniest when it's told in the right setting.

FOOTBALL TERMS TO KNOW

blitz (BLITS)—a play in which several defending players charge toward the quarterback to tackle him

center (SEN-tur)—the player who snaps the ball to the quarterback to start a play

chop block (CHOP BLOK)—an illegal block aimed at the legs and knees of another player

fair catch (FAYR KACH)—a catch of a kicked football by a player who gives a signal; the player may not advance the ball or be tackled by the defense

gridiron (GRID-eye-ruhn)—another word for a football field

huddle (HUHD-uhl)—a gathering of players on the football field before a play

nickelback (NICK-uhl-bak)—a cornerback or safety who serves as the fifth defensive player in the backfield

pancake block (PAN-cake BLOK)—when an offensive line player knocks a defender to the ground

pass interference (PASS in-tur-FIHR-uhnss)—an illegal move to block an opposing player from catching the ball

penalty (PEN-uhl-tee)—a punishment for breaking the rules

roughing (RUFF-ing)—a penalty in which a defensive player makes illegal contact with the quarterback after he has thrown a pass

sack (SAK)—when a defensive player tackles the opposing quarterback behind the line of scrimmage

GLOSSARY

arachnid (uh-RAK-nihd)—a group of animals that includes spiders, scorpions, mites, and ticks

electrolyte (ih-LEK-truh-lyt)—a substance that helps regulate nutrients and balance fluids in the body

hibernate (HYE-bur-nate)—to spend the winter in a deep sleep

mammal (MAM-uhl)—a warm-blooded animal that breathes air; mammals have hair or fur and feed milk to their young

prospector (PRAH-spek-tuhr)—a person who looks for valuable minerals such as silver or gold

ABOUT THE AUTHOR

John Sazaklis is a *New York Times* bestselling author of more than 100 children's books. He has also illustrated Spider-Man books, created toys for *MAD Magazine*, and written for the BEN 10 animated series. John lives in New York City with his wonderful wife and dynamic daughter.

READ THEM ALL!

JAKE MADDOX SPORTS JOKES

GUT-BUSTING
BASKETBALL
JOKES AND PUNS

JAKE MADDOX SPORTS JOKES

HILARIOUS
DANCE, CHEER, AND GYMNASTICS
JOKES AND PUNS

JAKE MADDOX SPORTS JOKES

LAUGH-OUT-LOUD
FOOTBALL
JOKES AND PUNS

JAKE MADDOX SPORTS JOKES

SIDE-SPLITTING
SOCCER
JOKES AND PUNS